What Is
the Constitution?

by Patricia Brennan Demuth

illustrated by Tim Foley

Penguin Workshop

For my constant coven: Val, Erica,
Ellen, Ann, Kathleen—PBD

PENGUIN WORKSHOP
An Imprint of Penguin Random House LLC, New York

Penguin supports copyright. Copyright fuels creativity, encourages diverse voices, promotes free speech, and creates a vibrant culture. Thank you for buying an authorized edition of this book and for complying with copyright laws by not reproducing, scanning, or distributing any part of it in any form without permission. You are supporting writers and allowing Penguin to continue to publish books for every reader.

The publisher does not have any control over and does not assume any responsibility for author or third-party websites or their content.

Visit us online at www.penguinrandomhouse.com.

Library of Congress Control Number: 2018010770

ISBN 9781524786090 (paperback)   10 9 8 7
ISBN 9781524786113 (library binding)   10 9 8 7 6 5 4 3

Contents

What Is the Constitution?

The first time the thirteen American colonies declared themselves a free nation was in the Declaration of Independence, written in July of 1776. By then, the colonies were fed up with being ruled from afar by Great Britain. A bloody war for independence broke out—the Revolutionary War.

At the start, winning the war seemed impossible. How could the ragtag rebel army ever defeat Great Britain, the mightiest military power in the world? But a fierce drive to be free fired the rebels' spirits.

By 1783, the war was over—and the colonies were no longer colonies. They were states in a free and independent nation: the United States of America!

Even while at war, the new country had needed some sort of government. So, in 1776, a group of leaders of the Revolution had quickly patched together some rules. They were called the Articles of Confederation.

Nobody wanted a government that was all-powerful. That's what the states were breaking away from. So, they created a congress that was too weak to do any harm. Unfortunately, the result was a government that was too weak to do much good, either.

By 1787, just four years after the United States' glorious victory, the young country was in trouble. National pride didn't exist yet. In fact, if you asked most people what their country was, they named their state. It was easy to see why.

Over their whole lifetime, people rarely traveled more than thirty miles away from where they were born. In 1785, a man from Georgia wrote that he was leaving his "country" to go to "a strange land amongst strangers." The "strange land" was New York!

States quarreled often over where their state boundary lines were and which state "owned" certain rivers. Enemies abroad smirked at America's troubles. Didn't all this arguing prove that the upstart nation was not capable of ruling itself without a powerful king?

America's young government needed fixing—and soon. So, during the horribly hot and sticky summer of 1787, fifty-five men from twelve states gathered in Philadelphia for a special meeting. (Rhode Island wouldn't come.) Their mission was to change the Articles of Confederation. Most had no idea they were going to frame—to plan out—a whole new system of government!

The framers, which is what history books call these men, had to find answers to big, thorny questions. Who decided if the United States would go to war again? What powers should be given to the head of the government? What should happen if leaders abused their power? Who should be allowed to vote? How would laws get passed?

For four months, the framers debated . . . and debated . . . and debated. Tempers flared. Voices rose. Every man cared deeply about his ideas. It was hard work to listen to the other side. So

much was at stake! They knew they were trying to decide the fate for "millions yet unborn," as delegate George Mason said.

At some points, writing a new constitution seemed hopeless. Would an agreement ever be reached?

CHAPTER 1
A Limping Government

In 1787, the United States of America had a name. And it had a flag. Yet many things were missing to make it a true nation.

There was no president. There was no central court system. Neither was there a US army or navy. There was no Senate or House of Representatives—only a weak "Congress." Congress could pass laws, but it could not enforce them. For instance, Congress could charge taxes to pay off war debts. But it had to rely on the goodwill of the states to pay up.

People's loyalty to their state made it hard for them to think of themselves as Americans. During the Revolution, George Washington asked soldiers from New Jersey to swear loyalty to America. What an odd request! They said that New Jersey was their country.

Loyalty to one's state was rooted in history. The thirteen colonies had been settled at different times by different groups of people. Each state developed its own way of life, often with its own religion and customs. Strict Puritans had settled New England. Peace-loving Quakers founded Pennsylvania.

Although the main language of the colonies was English, tens of thousands spoke German in Pennsylvania. Shopkeepers and fishermen thrived in New England, whereas the South was mainly agricultural.

The Articles of Confederation held the states together well enough to fight the war. But afterward, each state was happy to go its own way again. Soldiers returned home. And each state got busy creating its own constitution and electing its own leaders.

But what about being a country? Some leaders (like George Washington, James Madison, and Alexander Hamilton) wanted the United States to be a strong nation with a solid central government, one that would oversee all the states. These leaders were called nationalists.

But other leaders wanted power to remain with the states, just as it did with the Articles of Confederation. The Articles promised that the states would remain sovereign. That meant each state was still its own boss. What about the union? The Articles described the union loosely, as a "league of friendship."

How well did this government work? Not too well. By 1787, America's troubles could fill a long list.

Alexander Hamilton (1755–1804)

Nobody fought harder for the Constitutional Convention than Alexander Hamilton. Born on an

island in the British West Indies, Alexander arrived in America as a teenager. Without strong roots in any state, Hamilton developed a grand vision for the nation as a whole.

Brilliant and fiery, Hamilton had played an important role in the American Revolution as an aide to George Washington. Hamilton attended the Constitutional Convention as a delegate from New York. Afterward, he served on President George Washington's first cabinet as Secretary of the Treasury. Hamilton's life was cut short in 1804 when Aaron Burr, the vice president, shot him in a duel.

Some states charged fees on goods bought in other states, as if they were foreign countries. Lands west of the original thirteen colonies were being settled, and disagreements broke out over which states controlled them.

Continental money was all but worthless. So, seven states printed their own paper money but it was no good outside of their boundaries.

George Washington, back home in Virginia, grew alarmed at what was happening to his country. Congress is "a half-starved, limping government," he complained, "always moving on crutches and tottering at every step."

Also, in 1786 a crisis broke out in western Massachusetts. Many poor farmers were losing their land because they couldn't pay their state's high taxes.

Under Daniel Shays, a former Revolutionary War captain, a mob of two thousand farmers decided to rebel. They marched to Springfield armed with axes, pitchforks, and old muskets.

The weak Congress couldn't put together an armed force. So, Massachusetts sent in its own troops and stopped the rebellion. In the end, four men lay dead.

Shays's Rebellion shook the nation. Americans were killing Americans! "I am mortified beyond expression," said George Washington. (*Mortified* means very, very embarrassed.)

Alexander Hamilton had this to say: "There is only one remedy—to call a convention of all the states, and the sooner the better." If the government wasn't made stronger, it could fall apart.

Even Congress agreed that the Articles of Confederation needed changes. So it asked the states to elect delegates to attend a special meeting in Philadelphia, in May of 1787. Newspapers called it the "Grand Convention." No one called it a Constitutional Convention, of course, because who knew that a whole new Constitution was about to be written?

CHAPTER 2
Who's Coming to Philadelphia?

In the spring
of 1787, fifty-five
delegates from twelve
states got ready to travel
to the Grand Convention
in Philadelphia.

Philadelphia prepared
a big welcome. It laid
out the red carpet—
or rather, *gravel*—in
front of the State
House where the Convention would be held. The
gravel was supposed to deaden the clack of noisy
carriage wheels over cobblestone streets so that
the delegates wouldn't be disturbed.

Philadelphia: A Historic City

In 1787, Philadelphia ranked as the nation's biggest city by far. The Declaration of Independence had been signed there at the State House—the very same spot where the Convention was being held. Small shops lined the downtown. Ships from around the world came and went from its busy Delaware River port. The city had streetlamps, thanks to its famous citizen Benjamin Franklin. Franklin also started America's first public library in Philadelphia.

State House

May 14 was the date the Convention was supposed to start. But hardly any of the fifty-five delegates made it there on time. The spring of 1787 was one of the wettest ever. Everywhere, stagecoaches and carriages got stuck in the muddy dirt roads.

Back then, even in good weather, travel was hard, slow, and bumpy. Vast areas of the country had no roads. Many rivers had no bridges. The trip from Georgia to Philadelphia took at least two to three weeks.

New Hampshire's delegates didn't arrive until July. But the weather was not entirely to blame. The state had a lot of trouble scraping up the money to send delegates!

One man, however, slipped quietly into town eleven days *early*. He was James Madison of Virginia. Madison was quiet, shy, and bookish. Today, he might be described as a "nerd." He stood just five feet three inches and weighed barely a hundred pounds. Someone once described him as "no bigger than a half piece of soap." Yet his giant intellect impressed all who knew him.

Lately, Madison had been poring over books about governments, both modern and ancient ones, in which the citizens governed themselves. Why did some governments fail and others succeed? Madison collected the best ideas, and then wrote out his own bold plan for government. It was tucked inside his bag. That

George Washington, 6' 2"   James Madison, 5' 3"

plan would end up becoming the blueprint for the United States! James Madison would play such an important role at the Convention that he became known as the "Father of the Constitution."

James Madison (1751–1836)

Like George Washington, James Madison grew up on a large plantation in Virginia. Poor health kept the young Madison from hunting and horseback riding. Instead, he spent hours in his father's library. By twelve, Madison could read French, Latin, and Greek.

With Thomas Jefferson as his mentor, Madison threw himself into politics. Under President Thomas Jefferson, he served two terms as Secretary of State. In 1809, Madison himself became the fourth president of the United States.

A day before the Convention, the great George Washington arrived! A military guard, dressed in spiffy uniforms and shiny black boots, welcomed him to town with cannon fire and gunfire. Cheering crowds lined the streets.

Since the end of the war, Washington had lived happily at his plantation in Virginia. However, a strong sense of duty now called Washington back to public life. He feared that all the bloodshed of the war would have been for nothing if the government didn't become stronger.

Mount Vernon

Washington's presence at the Convention was all-important. His steady leadership made other delegates willing to listen to differing opinions.

By May 25, men from seven states were present—enough to get started. The men gathering in the State House met six days a week, from ten o'clock to three or four o'clock.

Who were they? They were all white men, most of whom were well-off and highly educated. Many were young, in their twenties or thirties. Yet every single one already had lots of experience in government. Several had signed the Declaration of Independence. Three-fourths had served in the old Congress. Many were battlefield heroes of the Revolution. They were a fashionable group, too, wearing breeches, silk stockings, and powdered white wigs.

Two important leaders were missing: Thomas Jefferson and John Adams. They were an ocean away, representing America's interests in France and England.

The oldest delegate by far was Benjamin Franklin, who lived right in Philadelphia. At eighty-one, Dr. Franklin still had a quick mind, but his body ached from gout. Bumpy carriage rides were too hard on him. So, he was brought into the Convention on a French sedan chair. Four prisoners, released from jail for the day, carried him in.

Benjamin Franklin (1706–1790)

Everyone called Benjamin Franklin "Doctor" because he had so many honorary degrees from universities. And yet, he had left school at age ten. In time, Benjamin Franklin became one of the great men of his age—an inventor, publisher, scientist, writer, and statesman. The first to discover that lightning was electricity, Ben Franklin "tamed the lightning" by inventing the lightning rod. He also invented bifocal glasses.

After the war, Franklin negotiated the United States' peace treaty with England.

Like George Washington, Ben Franklin brought a sense of calm and dignity to the Convention. In the coming months, as tempers rose, everyone would need that.

CHAPTER 3
Virginia Has a Plan

For the next four months, delegates walked or rode each morning to the State House. Before going inside, they were stopped by prisoners begging at the jail just behind it. The prisoners would push their caps out the windows on long "begging poles" and insult any man who didn't drop in coins.

The scene inside the grand, two-story brick building was more serene. The delegates met in the East Room. It was forty feet square with a looming ceiling twenty feet high. Tall windows and two marble fireplaces graced the sides. Scattered about the room were tables covered in smooth green felt.

James Madison always seated himself at the front of the room—the prime spot to hear everything that was said. He'd decided to write down everything discussed in the debates. For the rest of the Convention, he furiously scribbled notes, dipping his quill pen in and out of ink all day long. At night in his room at an inn, he carefully rewrote them. His important record of events became a treasure to historians. It's a special inside look into the framers' minds and what happened day by day.

The Convention's first order of business was to elect a chairman. Every single delegate voted for George Washington. Washington stepped to the front of the room and took his seat on a low platform facing everybody else. For the rest of the Convention, he would say little. His job was to keep the meetings on course.

Next, the delegates set two important rules for themselves. First, they decided to keep their meetings secret. No one was to breathe a word about the Convention outside the room— not even to family or friends. To enforce the rule, a guard was placed outside the door. And the windows were sealed shut. During the hot, steamy summer ahead, framers sweated in coats and vests. The New England gentlemen wearing wool suffered the most. Still, the windows stayed closed.

Why all the secrecy? The delegates wanted to speak their minds freely without worrying about anything landing in newspapers.

Second, the delegates set a rule that allowed them to change their minds on issues after a first vote. Some questions (such as the number of congressional seats per state) were so difficult that delegates needed to debate them over and over. After each debate, a vote was taken to see where everyone stood. But the votes weren't final. This system kept delegates from leaving the Convention when their side lost a vote. (At different times, more than half the men threatened to walk out!) By sticking around, a man might still persuade others to his way of thinking—and win the next vote.

The real work of creating a new government began on the fourth day. James Madison had already written up a plan. He figured that the first one introduced would get the most attention. And he was right.

Madison's voice was quiet and squeaky. So, Madison asked another delegate from Virginia, Edmund Randolph, to deliver the plan. Randolph

Edmund Randolph

was Virginia's tall, young governor. From then on, Madison's ideas became known as "the Virginia Plan."

The Virginia Plan called for three branches of government: *legislative*, *executive*, and *judicial*.

The legislative branch, the Congress, was made up of elected members. It would make the laws for the nation. Congress was to be split into two groups, or houses, a bigger one and a smaller one. Today, the bigger house is called the House of Representatives; the smaller house is the Senate.

The executive branch, headed by some kind of president, would carry out the laws. And the judicial branch, led by a Supreme Court was to interpret the laws, deciding whether or not they were fair.

What was the point of having three different branches? Madison thought that, with different duties spread out, no single branch could ever seize too much power. The other branches would be able to step in and stop that from happening. This system of controls is known as "checks and balances."

When Randolph finished reading the Virginia Plan, no one seemed too upset . . . at least not until he explained the plan in his own way. Randolph used the explosive word *national*.

Soon, his meaning sank in. A national government would undercut the power of the states! (In the Congress that the Articles of Confederation set up, members had answered to state governments.)

Utter silence fell over the room when Randolph sat down. One long minute passed, then another,

as delegates sat stunned. Only a few of them had considered creating a new national government. Most had come to the Convention expecting to revise (change) the Articles of Confederation—not scrap them altogether! Finally, the silence broke—and the arguing began. It wouldn't stop for weeks.

CHAPTER 4
Small Versus Big

The small states hated the Virginia Plan! The rule in the former Congress had always been "one state, one vote." So all states—whether big or small—had equal power. But the Virginia Plan would change that. It based each state's number of representatives on population. The more people a state had, the more representatives it would send to Congress.

Small states insisted they would *never* go along with this. They'd be "swallowed up" by big states such as Pennsylvania. Delegates from the small state of Delaware seemed ready to walk out at any minute.

Big states were just as stubborn: It made sense for states with more people to have more representatives. Arguing went on for days.

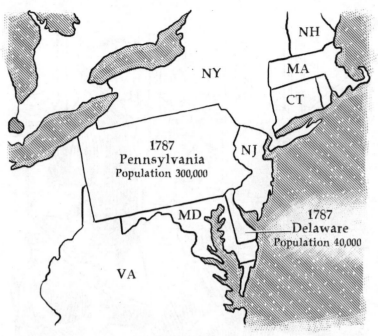

Then a group of small states decided it was time to form a new plan of their own. Led by the hardworking William Paterson of New Jersey, they worked at night to create "the New Jersey Plan." It called for a federation of states, not a strong national government. Congress would still have just one house. And each state would have an equal number of representatives. Sound familiar? It was.

James Madison stood up and ripped apart Paterson's New Jersey Plan. It had the same problems as the Articles of Confederation, he said. Such a government had already failed Americans. And it would let them down again.

The majority of the delegates agreed with Madison: The New Jersey Plan wouldn't work. On June 19, it was voted down. That left only the Virginia Plan—the one that called for a new central government. Now it was clear the delegates weren't just improving the Articles. They were creating a whole new constitution! In the history of the world, this had never happened. Men had never sat in a room to create a government from scratch! Could this grand experiment work?

Just because the New Jersey Plan was voted down, that didn't mean the small states were giving in. They were still determined to have equal representation in Congress.

Delegates from the big states tried everything to get the small states to change their minds. James Madison pointed out that the aim of the Virginia Plan was *not* to put the big states in charge. The goal was to give power to all the people.

Gouverneur Morris from Pennsylvania took a farsighted approach. In the future, he said, people would think of themselves as *Americans* first, not as citizens of a state.

The small states simply wouldn't budge—and neither would the big states. A lot of delegates were ready to sink the Convention rather than give in.

On the last Saturday of June, the delegates walked to the State House in sweltering heat. Buzzing bluebottle flies dive-bombed around their heads.

That morning, the Convention sank to its lowest point. Gunning Bedford, from the small state of Delaware, fumed, "I do not, gentlemen,

trust you!" He said that "foreign powers" such as France would be happy to help out the small states. Was Bedford hinting that soon there could be civil war in the United States?

Rufus King of Massachusetts charged that the small states were acting "vicious." He insisted he would *never* adopt "an equality of votes."

George Washington's face looked grim as he left the State House that day. The Convention was "held together by the strength of a hair," said Luther Martin of Maryland.

Fortunately, Sunday was a day off. On Monday, the delegates voted again on the Virginia Plan. Every man must have held his breath as the votes came in. The final tally: five states voted *yea*, five states voted *nay*, and one vote was a split vote. So it was a tie . . . a *deadlock*. (Remember: New Hampshire delegates didn't arrive until July.)

What could be done now? The delegates didn't want to give up. They felt "the eyes of the world [were] upon them." To save the Convention, they chose a committee, made up of one person from each state, to try and solve the problem.

Ten days later, after a break over the July Fourth holiday, the committee reported back. They thought they had a solution! The House of Representatives would be based on population. That's what the big states wanted. The Senate, however, would have two members from each state. That pleased the small states. And it would take both houses to pass any laws.

Called the Great Compromise, it was accepted by the delegates and written into the Constitution. A man named Roger Sherman from Connecticut was the brains behind it.

Roger Sherman

Ever since then, it's dictated how Congress is set up. Today, there are still two Senators from every state. The House of Representatives now has 435 members. California, the state with the most people, has fifty-three representatives. Wyoming, which is big in terms of land but has the smallest population, has only one representative.

Today we look at paintings of the framers of the Constitution dressed up in white powdered

wigs, knee britches, and buckled shoes. Because they all sort of looked alike, it's easy for us to assume they all thought alike.

That was far from the truth! With such huge differences of opinion, it's astounding that they ever reached the Great Compromise.

CHAPTER 5
A Battle Between North and South

Was the arguing over now?

Definitely not.

The delegates had settled that population would determine how many members each state would have in the House of Representatives. However, there was the terrible issue of slavery to take into account.

At the time, there were about half a million people in bondage in the United States, almost all of them living in the Southern states. Southern plantation owners depended on slaves' unpaid labor to farm their fields of tobacco, rice, and cotton.

Slaves had no rights. They were considered property, not citizens of the country. They couldn't vote. Yet if they were counted in a Southern state's population, that state would get many more representatives in the House of Representatives.

Of course, that's what Southern states wanted.

States with gradual or full emancipation by 1787

However, the thought of Southern states gaining more power in Congress because of their slaves made Northern delegates furious. Many of them hated slavery and spoke out against it. Even several framers who were slaveholders (including George Washington and James Madison) hoped slavery would end. Luther Martin of Maryland declared that the "dishonorable" slave trade went against the "principles of the Revolution." George Mason of Virginia said slavery brought the "judgment of heaven [down] on a country." Slavery also went against the

Luther Martin

Declaration of Independence, which declared that "all men are created equal."

But Southern delegates made it clear that they would leave the Convention if the new Constitution outlawed slavery. And without the South, there would be no nation, much less no Constitution.

So the issue was whether slaves should be counted as part of a state's population.

Once again, the delegates struck a compromise. They agreed that the Constitution would say that each enslaved person was counted as only three-fifths of a person.

If you read the Constitution, the word *slaves* never appears. The delegates avoided using it on purpose. Confusing words such as "other persons" were used instead. "[The word *slavery* was] hid away in the Constitution," said the sixteenth president, Abraham Lincoln, "just as an afflicted man hides away . . . a cancer, which he dares not cut out at once, lest he bleed to death."

Abraham Lincoln

The compromise over slavery kept the Convention alive and made it possible to have a Constitution. Delegates who hated slavery felt their hands were tied. Yet the Constitution, so successful in other ways, utterly failed African Americans in bondage.

Slavery After 1787

The Constitution also stated that the slave trade had to end in 1808. But that only meant that no new slaves would be brought into the country. By 1808, however, there were more than four million enslaved people in the United States.

The issue of slavery never went away and kept splitting North and South further and further apart. Finally, the United States did break apart in the Civil War (1861–1865). The Union won the war, and slavery was forever banned.

CHAPTER 6
Decisions, Decisions

Should a twenty-year-old or a foreigner be head of the US government? What should be done if that leader acts badly and breaks laws? Do ordinary citizens know enough to vote for a president? How long should members of Congress serve? Should Supreme Court justices keep their jobs for life? Decisions, decisions!

The framers had so many questions to debate in order to put together a brand-new government—even once the central issues were solved through compromises. Today, you can see their answers in action in our government.

In its eleven years as a country, the United States hadn't had anyone in charge. But that had led to problems. A leader was needed to command the armed forces, to deal with foreign nations, to guide the United States in an emergency. The delegates were willing to have a strong head—but not *too* strong. No kings or tyrants wanted!

For this reason, some delegates were afraid of having just one person at the head of government. It sounded too much like a ruler. They suggested *three* executives, one from each part of the country. After days of debate, the delegates decided there would be just one head of the nation, to be called "president." The president had to be at least thirty-five years old and born in the United States. (America's youngest presidents have been Theodore Roosevelt, 42, and John F. Kennedy, 43.)

Although the president would be named commander in chief, could he act on his own to declare war on an enemy? No. The delegates believed that decision was too important for just

Theodore Roosevelt, 42   John F. Kennedy, 43

one person to make. Only Congress could send the nation into war.

A president could propose (suggest) laws but not make laws. That was the job of Congress. But the framers did give the president a special power to veto (say: VEE-toe). Veto means the president stops a bill sent from Congress by refusing to sign it.

How a Law Is Made

The way Congress passes a law is spelled out in the Constitution. A law begins with a proposal, or a bill. Either house of Congress can introduce it.

If the House introduces the bill, then its members study it. Usually, they add changes. After voting for it, they send it to the Senate.

Senators study the bill. They make changes, too. After voting for it, they send it to the president. If the president signs the bill, it's a law!

OR . . .

The president vetoes the bill: He refuses to sign it. He sends it back to Congress.

Congress can still pass the bill, but now it's harder. They need to gather many more votes. But if they succeed, the president can't veto it again.

King George III

Who should choose the president? This was the hardest decision of all. At that time, most countries around the world did not elect their leader. Kings and queens ruled. And rule was passed down through a royal family from one generation to the next.

At the Convention, delegates made lots of different suggestions:

The Senate should choose the president!

No, the state legislatures should choose!

How about the state governors?

Then there was one really wild idea. What if the people elected their most important leader? The *people*? This notion caused the biggest uproar. Some delegates thought that ordinary citizens were too "ignorant" to make such an important decision. It would be like a blind man trying to pick colors, George Mason said.

James Wilson of Pennsylvania, however, argued strongly for the people's case: Since the president represented the American people, they should be the ones to elect him.

Still, the idea seemed impractical. The nation was huge—twelve hundred miles from north to south. How could voters down in Georgia learn about candidates up in New York? News traveled very slowly and was hard to get. Newspapers were just a few pages long and came out only once a week—plus only cities had them. Rough frontier towns to the west often got news that was a month old.

The delegates circled the nagging questions again and again. Sixty times votes were taken on how the president should be chosen! In the end, they voted for the people. But a very complicated system was set up to do it. It's called the electoral college.

Once a president was elected, how long should he serve? "For life!" said Alexander Hamilton. Other suggestions were seven, eleven, and fifteen years. Finally, the delegates settled on a president's term being four years. But he could be reelected again and again. (In 1951, the Twenty-Second Amendment put a limit on terms—a president can only be elected twice.)

What if a president dies in office or becomes very ill? What then? The delegates created the role of a vice president—someone who may counsel the president and be second in line to take over, if necessary. (During our history, this has happened nine times. The most recent was when Vice President Gerald Ford took over after President Richard Nixon resigned in 1974.)

The Electoral College

Today, citizens of each state elect their senators, US representatives, governors, and many other officials by direct popular vote: The candidate who gets the most votes wins the election. But to elect a president, there is a very complicated system. Even though citizens cast a ballot for the candidate of their choice, they are voting indirectly for the president. Each state has a certain number of electors (chosen by the political parties of that state)—and *their* vote for president is what counts. This complicated system can result in a president taking office whom the majority of Americans did not vote for. (Recently, this was the case both in 2000, when Al Gore lost the presidency to George W. Bush, and then again in 2016, when Donald Trump was elected president instead of Hillary Clinton.)

The delegates also gave the vice president a day-to-day job: presiding over the Senate. If there's a tie vote, the vice president breaks the tie.

An elected president might turn out to be bad or reckless. If that happens, the Constitution could take action. The president could be removed from office. How? First the House of Representatives votes to impeach him. Then there's a trial in the Senate. (So far, only two presidents—Andrew Johnson and Bill Clinton—have been impeached, but neither was removed from office.)

Andrew Johnson   Bill Clinton

When the delegates turned their attention to the Supreme Court, decisions were easier to make. Delegates were very familiar with how courts worked. About half were lawyers themselves.

They set up a Supreme Court with nine judges to act something like referees. (You can think of the judicial system being set up like a triangle: lots of local courts at the bottom, higher courts in the middle that might overturn the rulings of lower courts, and then a Supreme Court at the very top.)

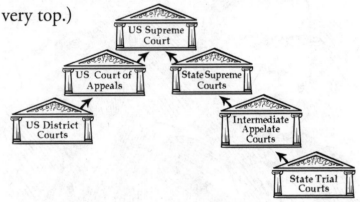

Only the most important cases reach the Supreme Court. It has the final say on any rule of law. It was important for Supreme Court judges to remain independent and never be swayed by the politics of the day—so the Constitution made sure they were appointed for life. They couldn't be removed just for making unpopular decisions.

Supreme Court, 2017

One of the last questions discussed was where the nation's new capital would be. All agreed that it shouldn't be part of any state. Instead, a special district, about ten miles square, would be set aside for the nation's capital. Where exactly?

The delegates decided not to pick the place! Let the new Congress do that, they agreed. (Washington, DC, became the nation's capital in 1790.)

Whew! The Convention was nearing its end.

Washington, DC: America's Capital

Three years after the Constitutional Convention, Washington, DC, became America's capital city. "DC" is short for District of Columbia (in honor of Christopher Columbus). Washington, DC, is the only city in America not in a state. Back in 1790, when there were only thirteen states, the new capital was right in the middle of the country—neither in the North nor in the South.

Washington, District of Columbia

United States of America in 1790

George Washington chose the site of the city named after him. It was to be built along the beautiful Potomac River. He himself never lived in the White House—the home of all other presidents—because it wasn't built in time.

Today, Washington, DC, is a city of historic landmarks. Atop a hill sits the home of Congress, the Capitol Building, with its massive dome. Nearby is the Lincoln Memorial, where Martin Luther King Jr. gave his famous "I Have a Dream" speech. One block from the Capitol is the Supreme Court Building, where the nine justices meet.

CHAPTER 7
"We the People"

The long, hot months of summer passed away. By September, cool breezes blew over Philadelphia rooftops. The important work at the Constitutional Convention was nearly done. For so long, delegates had been hard at work. Now they were restless to go home and rejoin their families.

On September 8, they handed over a draft of the Constitution to a Committee of Style. The committee's job was to polish the writing and put the whole thing together in readable form.

The committee chose Gouverneur Morris to write the final draft. Morris streamlined the Constitution into seven articles (sections). He untangled confusing sentences and trimmed

away unnecessary words. He also changed the very first sentence. The original draft began, "We the people of the states of New Hampshire, Massachusetts, Rhode Island . . ." It listed every state by name. The new opening simply read:

We the people of the United States . . .

By not naming each separate state, Morris signaled the dawn of a new government—one that answered directly to the people. It was a brilliant touch. The rest of the introduction told why the Constitution was written. Today, the introduction is known as the Preamble.

After just four days, the committee delivered the final draft of the Constitution. Delegates changed a few details. Then the document was sent out to be engrossed on parchment, high-quality thick paper.

Portrait of Alexander Hamilton

Portrait of James Madison, the "Father of the Constitution"

Portrait of Roger Sherman, who came up with the Great Compromise

The Assembly Room of Independence Hall
(Pennsylvania's State House)

A replica of George Washington's seat at the Grand Convention

Portrait of Gouverneur Morris, who helped write
the final draft of the Constitution

The inauguration of George Washington as
the first president of the United States

Members of the first cabinet of the United States
with George Washington (on right)

Bettmann/Getty Images

Suffragettes celebrate the passing of the Nineteenth Amendment, 1920

First draft of the Bill of Rights

The preamble to the US Constitution is etched on a wall of the National Constitution Center in Philadelphia.

Painting of the signing of the Constitution that hangs
in the United States Capitol Building

US Capitol Building

The Declaration of Independence, the Constitution, and the Bill of Rights
on display at the National Archives in Washington, DC

On September 17, thirty-nine delegates gathered in the State House one last time. (Some delegates had already been called home. Four had left in protest.) The framers lined up to sign the Constitution, spread out on the front table. George Washington signed first.

As Benjamin Franklin waited his turn, he gazed at a half sun that was carved into the back of George Washington's chair. All summer long, Franklin had wondered if the sun was rising or setting. Now he said he knew the answer. It was a rising sun, he happily declared.

The new day in America couldn't dawn just yet, however. The American people had to ratify the Constitution. (Ratify means "approve.") Only then would it become the law of the land.

Copies of the Constitution were sent out to all thirteen states. Newspapers printed every word. Soon the nation was abuzz with talk about government. Every class of people debated: frontiersmen, farmers, shopkeepers, landowners, and bankers. Citizens spoke their minds at town meetings and churches. They wrote editorials, pamphlets, and songs. Historians say it was the greatest outpouring of political thinking in western history.

Americans split into two groups, pro and con. Meanwhile, a series of articles in favor of the Constitution began showing up in New York newspapers. They were written under the pen name Publius. The "mystery writer" was really three people: Alexander Hamilton, James Madison, and John Jay. Their eighty-five essays are now known as the *Federalist Papers*.

The *Federalist Papers* calmed people's worries of an all-powerful government. They pointed out the safeguards planted in the Constitution— the system of checks and balances. If Congress passed bad laws, the president could veto them. If a president overstepped his powers, the Supreme Court could rule his acts "unconstitutional" and make him stop.

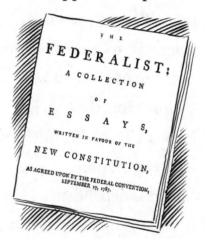

One by one, states called special conventions to ratify the Constitution—or not. Nine of the thirteen states had to approve the Constitution for it to become law. And on June 21, it happened. New Hampshire became the ninth state to ratify the Constitution! Five days later, Virginia, the largest state, ratified, too! "It is done. We have become a nation," declared

Benjamin Rush, who had been a signer of the Declaration of Independence. America had a new government—one that is now almost 250 years old. The bold experiment worked!

In time, all of the thirteen states ratified the Constitution—even those who had voted "no" at first. (Rhode Island, which had refused to send delegates to the Constitution, was the last to ratify, in May 1790.)

July Fourth was just two weeks away. The joyous city of Philadelphia got ready for a big-time celebration.

On Independence Day, 1788, the first cannon fired at sunrise in Philadelphia. Thousands of

people began pouring into the city center to celebrate the brand-new Constitution of the United States. At 9:30 a.m., a parade set off. A float with a towering blue eagle was followed by a giant framed Constitution. Next came ten white horses pulling a fancy dome on thirteen columns, one for each state.

Then came citizens from all walks of life. There were 200 metalworkers, 300 rope makers, and 450 carpenters. There were women spinning cloth, smithies making nails. Lawyers, soldiers, boat pilots, painters, porters, bricklayers, tailors,

coopers, saddlers, candle makers, butchers, and stonecutters. On and on they came.

The day ended with a picnic for seventeen thousand! What a celebration for "we the people of the United States."

CHAPTER 8
The Bill of Rights

The United States held its first elections under the new Constitution in 1789. George Washington became president—of course. The vote was unanimous! That would never happen again.

The new Congress started work on March 4, 1789. What was their first order of business? To change the Constitution!

While it was being ratified, several states had demanded that a bill of rights be added to the Constitution. A bill of rights is a list that guarantees people's basic freedoms.

So, the new Congress set about writing ten amendments—changes—to the Constitution. Who was chosen to write them? James Madison, the Father of the Constitution. The states approved ten of the amendments that Madison wrote. We call those ten amendments the Bill of Rights.

They list personal freedoms for all Americans—freedoms that no one can take away because the Constitution protects them. To many, the Bill of Rights is the heart of the Constitution.

The First Amendment is a gold mine of liberties. It protects five important rights: freedom of religion; freedom of speech; freedom of the press; freedom to assemble; and freedom to ask the government to correct wrongs.

Freedom of religion wasn't common back in 1787. Several states had state churches. Tax money paid for them. Even people of different faiths had to pay for the state church. In Massachusetts, only Christians were allowed to run for office. Virginia threw Baptists in jail for preaching. The First Amendment ordered states to get rid of these old religious laws.

Today, many countries still tell their people what religion to follow. But, in America, people can worship any way they please—or not at all.

Christians, Jews, Muslims, Buddhists, and atheists (people who do not believe in the existence of God) all share equal rights. The First Amendment says so.

Freedom of speech and press means that people can voice their opinions in newspapers, speeches, books, and on TV and the Internet. No one can be punished for speaking their beliefs, even if the government doesn't like what someone says. (Of course, there are limits on free speech. For example, falsely yelling "Fire!" in a crowded movie theater is a crime.)

Under British rule, American colonists were sometimes arrested for disagreeing with the king. And today, around the world, harsh governments still lock up citizens who challenge leaders. But, in the United States, different points of view keep democracy strong.

Can large groups also protest? The First Amendment says yes. People can gather together in large numbers to show resistance to their leaders and laws—just as long as they protest peacefully.

In the 1950s and 1960s, African American leaders, like Martin Luther King Jr., led thousands and thousands of protestors in peaceful marches. The power of the Civil Rights Movement brought about important changes for racial justice.

The Second Amendment protects the right of people to own arms. Arms are weapons, such as guns. Why would the Constitution protect gun ownership? The reason given in the Second Amendment is to keep militias well-armed. Militias (say: mi-LISH-uhs) were small armies of citizen-soldiers. During the Revolution, militias could quickly gather in case of attack by British soldiers.

Today there are no militias; states have National Guard troops instead. But the Second Amendment still protects the right of Americans to own guns.

Millions of gun owners want to safeguard their Second Amendment right. Millions of others point to the shocking gun violence in the

United States. The weapons of the 1700s were muskets and rifles. They argue that the framers of the Constitution never imagined automatic weapons being carried on city streets. They want restrictions on who can own weapons, how they can buy them, and what kinds of weapons can be bought.

Half of the amendments in the Bill of Rights protect people accused of crimes. They make sure that arrests and trials are fair, and that the rights of the accused are protected.

Americans suspected of a crime have other rights, too. Let's say the police think someone is hiding stolen goods in their house. The police cannot come and do a search without a warrant (a written permission) from a judge.

The Eighth Amendment says that a convicted criminal cannot receive "cruel and unusual punishment." What does that mean? People's ideas about that have changed over time. The colonists often punished people by locking them in public stocks, sometimes for days. Beatings or floggings with a whip were common, too. Now, these punishments seem very cruel to us.

Some countries around the globe give harsh punishments. They might stone criminals to death, or cut off the hands of thieves. The US Constitution does not permit such cruel acts.

Today, the debate about "cruel and unusual punishment" in America revolves around the death penalty. Some states still put criminals who commit the most severe crimes to death. Nineteen states, however, have passed laws making the death penalty illegal. They believe that putting someone to death—even if it's done in the most painless way possible—is always "cruel and unusual punishment."

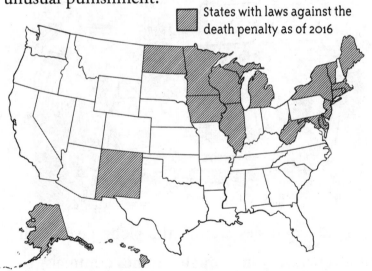

States with laws against the death penalty as of 2016

The Bill of Rights was the first major addition to the Constitution—but certainly not the last.

CHAPTER 9
The Living Constitution

The US Constitution was far from finished in 1789. The founders knew that every generation of Americans would face new changes—changes the founders couldn't foresee. So, they made sure that future citizens could control and change their government. One way is by adding more amendments. Since the Bill of Rights, seventeen other amendments have been added to the Constitution.

Some amendments right the wrongs of the past. Slavery was a burning injustice left standing when the Constitution was first written. The issue led to the Civil War (1861–1865). Upon the victory of the North, the Thirteenth Amendment (1865) was passed, outlawing slavery everywhere in the United States. Later, the Fourteenth and Fifteenth Amendments granted equal protection under the law to all citizens in 1868, and voting rights to all men in 1870.

Thirteenth Amendment

It wasn't until 1920, with the passing of the Nineteenth Amendment, that voting rights were given to another huge group of Americans: women.

There have been thousands of attempts to amend the Constitution. But it's very hard to do. Two-thirds of the House and Senate have to agree on a new amendment. Then three-quarters of the states also have to pass it.

Women's Right to Vote

The fight for women's right to vote had started back in the mid-1800s. Leading the way were many activists—Elizabeth Cady Stanton, Lucretia Mott, Sojourner Truth, and Susan B. Anthony. The first

Elizabeth Cady Stanton, Lucretia Mott, and Sojourner Truth

women's rights convention took place in Seneca Falls, New York, in 1848. There was a written declaration, modeled on the Declaration of Independence. It said that "all men and women are created equal." Still, by 1910, only five states had guaranteed women the right to vote.

During World War I (1914–1918), hundreds of thousands of women joined the workforce for the first time to fill jobs left by men fighting overseas. Afterward, the fight for women's suffrage grew stronger. (Suffrage means the right to vote in an election.) Activists staged huge parades, marches, and pickets. At last, in 1919, Congress passed the Nineteenth Amendment, guaranteeing women the right to vote nationwide. It was approved in 1920.

Over the course of the country's history, situations have arisen that have brought to life every point that the framers debated. Eight presidents died or were assassinated in office.

Zachary
Taylor
1850

William Henry
Harrison
1841

Abraham
Lincoln
1865
(assassinated)

James A.
Garfield
1881
(assassinated)

Because of the Constitution, vice presidents were ready to step into office and keep our government running smoothly.

Warren G.
Harding
1923

William
McKinley
1901
(assassinated)

Franklin D.
Roosevelt
1945

John F.
Kennedy
1963
(assassinated)

The framers hoped the Constitution was strong enough to hold up the government in difficult times. And it has. The Constitution—that amazing four-page document—created the longest-living democratic government ever known.

You can see the original signed copy of the Constitution on display at the National Archives in Washington, DC. The ink of George Washington's signature has hardly faded. And at the top, embossed in huge, flowing script, are the words that include all Americans: "We the people."

Where Is the Original Constitution?

In Washington, DC, the National Archives Building displays the original copy of the Constitution, as well as the Bill of Rights and the Declaration of Independence. There is also a National Archives Museum with many exhibits and documents about the founding of the United States.

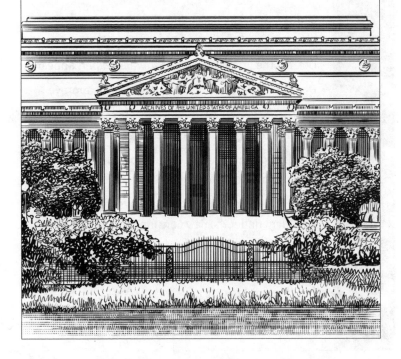

Timeline of the US Constitution

1787 — May 25: Enough delegates arrive for the Constitutional Convention to begin

— May 29: The Virginia Plan, based on James Madison's ideas, is presented

— July 13: The Confederation Congress passes the Northwest Ordinance, keeping new territories free of slavery

— July 16: Delegates accept the Great Compromise, settling the matter of representation in Congress

— Sept. 12: Final draft of the Constitution is presented

— Sept. 17: At the final meeting, thirty-nine delegates sign the new Constitution

— Oct. 27: The first essay of the *Federalist Papers* appears

— Dec. 7: Delaware becomes the first state to approve the new Constitution

1788 — June 21: The US Constitution becomes law

— July 4: Huge celebrations of the Constitution take place throughout the nation

1789 — Apr. 30: George Washington becomes the first US president under the new Constitution

1865 — The Thirteenth Amendment abolishes slavery

1870 — The Fifteenth Amendment gives African American men the right to vote

Timeline of the World

c. 400 BC —	The Greek city-state of Athens establishes the first democracy
1607 —	The first successful English settlement in North America is founded at Jamestown
1681 —	The Pennsylvania Colony is founded by William Penn
1732 —	The colony of Georgia is founded and named after King George II
1760 —	King George III ascends England's throne; he rules during the American Revolution
1776 —	On July 4, the thirteen colonies declare independence from England in the Declaration of Independence
1777 —	The Continental Congress adopts the Articles of Confederation; the states ratify them in 1781
1786 —	Daniel Shays leads a tax revolt
1803 —	President Thomas Jefferson doubles the size of the United States through the Louisiana Purchase
1809 —	James Madison is elected fourth US president
1814 —	British troops set fire to the White House during the War of 1812
1861 —	Southern states leave the Union, starting the Civil War
1963 —	Martin Luther King Jr. gives his "I Have a Dream" speech during the March on Washington
1974 —	President Richard Nixon resigns from office

Bibliography

*Books for young readers

Bowen, Catherine Drinker. *Miracle at Philadelphia: The Story of the Constitutional Convention, May to September 1787.* Boston: Little, Brown and Company, 1966.

Collier, Christopher, and James Lincoln Collier. *Decision in Philadelphia: The Constitutional Convention of 1787.* New York: Ballantine Books, 2007.

*Fritz, Jean. *Shh! We're Writing the Constitution.* New York: Puffin Books, 1997.

*Harris, Michael C. *What Is the Declaration of Independence?* New York: Penguin Workshop, 2016.

*Levy, Elizabeth. *If You Were There When They Signed the Constitution.* New York: Scholastic Inc., 1987.

*Maestro, Betsy, and Giulio Maestro. *A More Perfect Union: The Story of Our Constitution.* New York: HarperCollins Publishers, 1987.

Stewart, David O. *The Summer of 1787: The Men Who Invented the Constitution.* New York: Simon & Schuster, 2007.